A Toasted Loaf for Dad

By Cameron Macintosh

“It’s Dad’s big day!” said Joe.

“Let’s make him lunch,”
said Moe.
“That will show him
that we love him!”

"We can make roast beef!" said Moe.

They got some beef.

"Do you know what to do with it?" said Joe.

“No, I do not know!” said Moe, with a low groan.

They both sat to think.

“We can poach a fish!” yelled Joe.

They got a fish.

"What do we do with it?" said Moe.

"I do not know!" said Joe, with woe.

“What can we make, Joe?” said Moe.

“Well, I know the way to make toast,” said Joe.

Joe got an oat loaf
from the box.

Moe got some goat's cheese.

Then they toasted the loaf.

“Let’s load up the toast
with goat’s cheese!” said Moe.

“Then we will go
and give it to Dad,” said Joe.

"Dad, we made toast for you!" yelled Moe and Joe.

They gave Dad the toasted loaf.

"Thank you!" said Dad.
"You two are so grown up!"

Moe and Joe glowed
with pride.

CHECKING FOR MEANING

1. What does Joe first suggest they make for Dad? *(Literal)*
2. What did Joe and Moe use to make the toast? *(Literal)*
3. How do you think Dad felt after Joe and Moe gave him the toast? *(Inferential)*

EXTENDING VOCABULARY

roast	How do you roast something? What equipment do you need? What are some foods that you might roast?
woe	What does it mean if you speak with woe? When might you feel woe? What word means the opposite of *woe*?
grown	What are the sounds in the word *grown*? What word in the text sounds the same as *grown* but is spelled differently?

MOVING BEYOND THE TEXT

1. What special days do you celebrate with your family, carers, classmates or friends?
2. What is your favourite topping to have on toast?
3. Joe and Moe also had apples, bananas and pears on their kitchen bench. How might they have used those fruits in a different recipe or dish?
4. Moe and Joe wanted to celebrate their dad. What are some other things you can do for people to show you care about them?

TIME TO WRITE

Write about some food you know how to make or prepare.

PRACTICE WORDS

Moe

show

roast

Joe

low

groan

know

no

toast

poach

go

woe

toasted

both

oat

goat's

loaf

grown

glowed

load

so